Siberian Tiger Fun Facts

Picture Book for Kids

MARILYN TRUELUCK

Physical characteristics

Siberian tigers are the largest of all tiger subspecies, with males weighing up to 660 pounds (300 kilograms).

Their fur is thick and insulating, with a beautiful orange coat marked by dark stripes that help them blend into their surroundings.

Siberian tigers have long, muscular bodies and strong limbs, enabling them to leap and pounce on their prey.

They have a distinctive white winter coat that helps them camouflage in the snow-covered forests of their habitat.

Their powerful jaws are filled with sharp teeth and strong muscles, allowing them to deliver a lethal bite to their prey.

Physical characteristics

Siberian tigers have excellent vision, which helps them spot prey from a distance.

They possess retractable claws that they use for hunting and climbing trees.

These magnificent cats have a strong sense of smell, allowing them to detect prey and mark their territory.

Their long, flexible tails help them maintain balance and serve as a communication tool.

Siberian tigers have large, round heads with prominent cheekbones and forward-facing eyes, giving them excellent depth perception.

Diet and feeding habits

Siberian tigers are carnivores and primarily prey on large ungulates, such as deer and wild boars.

They are capable of taking down prey that is much larger than themselves.

Siberian tigers are opportunistic hunters and will also eat smaller animals like rabbits and fish.

A single tiger can consume up to 88 pounds (40 kilograms) of meat in one feeding.

They are ambush predators, relying on stealth and surprise to catch their prey.

Diet and feeding habits

After making a successful kill, Siberian tigers will often drag their prey to a secluded area to consume it.

These tigers are known to be patient hunters, waiting for the perfect moment to strike.

Siberian tigers have strong teeth and jaws that allow them to bite through bones and tear into tough hides.

They are skilled swimmers and will often pursue prey into the water.

Siberian tigers have been observed caching their kills and returning to them later for a meal.

Behavior and social life

Siberian tigers are solitary animals, with adults usually maintaining large home ranges.

Males have larger territories than females and will mark their boundaries with scent markings and claw marks on trees.

They are mostly nocturnal, hunting and patrolling their territories during the cover of darkness.

Siberian tigers are known for their ability to cover vast distances within their territories.

They are agile climbers and will often retreat to the safety of trees to rest or to scan their surroundings.

Behavior and social life

During mating Season, males will vocalize and mark their territories to attract females.

Female tigers have overlapping home ranges with other females, but they are highly territorial and will defend their territory from intruders.

Siberian tigers are generally solitary, except during mating or when a female is raising her cubs.

They have a complex system of Scent marking, using urine and scratch marks to communicate with other tigers.

Siberian tigers are known to be excellent swimmers and will swim across rivers and lakes in search of prey or to find new territories.

HABITAT AND RANGE

Siberian tigers are found primarily in the remote forests of eastern Russia, particularly in the region of Siberia.

They inhabit a variety of habitats, including dense forests, taiga, and mountainous areas.

These tigers require large home ranges to find enough prey to sustain themselves.

The Amur-Heilong region, which spans Russia and China, is one of the last strongholds for Siberian tigers.

Their range used to extend into North Korea, but due to habitat loss and poaching, they are now limited to Russia and a small population in northeast China.

HABITAT AND RANGE

Siberian tigers are adapted to living in cold climates and are able to withstand harsh winters.

They prefer habitats with dense vegetation that provides cover for hunting and protection.

Siberian tigers are known to roam across vast distances, with some individuals traveling hundreds of miles in search of food or mates.

Human encroachment and habitat fragmentation are major threats to the survival of Siberian tigers.

Conservation efforts, such as protected areas and anti-poaching measures, are crucial for preserving their habitat and ensuring their survival.

REPRODUCTION AND FAMILY LIFE

FeMaLe SIBERIAN TiGeRs REACH SEXUAL MaTURiTy AROUND THE AGE OF 3-4 yeaRs, WHiLe MaLes MATURE aRoUND 4-5 yeaRs.

MATING TypicaLLy occURs DURING THE WiNTeR MoNTHs, WiTH A GESTATION peRioD OF aBoUT 3-3.5 MoNTHs.

A FeMaLe WILL GiVe BIRTH To A LiTTeR oF 2-4 cUBs, UsUaLLy iN A DEN HiDDeN IN DeNse VeGeTaTioN oR A caVe.

THe CUBS ARE BoRN BLiND aND HELPLESS, ReLyiNG oN THEIR MoTHeR FoR WaRMTH aND NoURisHMeNT.

THe MoTHeR Raises THe cUBs aLoNe, pROViDiNG THeM WiTH MILK AND TeacHiNG THeM iMpoRTaNT HUNTiNG AND SURViVaL SKILLS.

REPRODUCTION AND FAMILY LIFE

CUBS START VENTURING OUT OF THE DEN WHEN THEY ARE ABOUT 2 MONTHS OLD, BUT THEY REMAIN DEPENDENT ON THEIR MOTHER FOR SEVERAL MORE MONTHS.

SIBERIAN TIGER CUBS DEVELOP QUICKLY, WITH THEIR DISTINCTIVE STRIPES STARTING TO FADE AS THEY GROW.

THE BOND BETWEEN A MOTHER AND HER CUBS IS STRONG, AND SHE WILL FIERCELY DEFEND THEM FROM ANY POTENTIAL THREATS.

CUBS STAY WITH THEIR MOTHER FOR ABOUT 2 YEARS BEFORE THEY BECOME INDEPENDENT AND VENTURE OUT TO ESTABLISH THEIR OWN TERRITORIES.

THE SURVIVAL RATE OF TIGER CUBS IS RELATIVELY LOW, WITH MANY FALLING VICTIM TO PREDATION OR OTHER FACTORS DURING THEIR EARLY YEARS.

HISTORY AND CONSERVATION

Siberian tigers, also known as Amur tigers, are the largest tiger subspecies and one of the most endangered big cats in the world.

They have faced severe population declines due to habitat loss, poaching, and human-wildlife conflict.

In the 1940s, the population of Siberian tigers was estimated to be as low as **20-30** individuals.

Thanks to conservation efforts, their numbers have increased, and the population is now estimated to be around **500** individuals in the wild.

The establishment of protected areas and anti-poaching measures has played a crucial role in their conservation.

HISTORY AND CONSERVATION

International cooperation between Russia and China has helped protect their shared habitat and ensure the survival of this subspecies.

Siberian tigers are listed as endangered by the International Union for Conservation of Nature (IUCN).

The Amur-Heilong region has been designated as a key conservation area for Siberian tigers, with efforts focused on preserving their habitat and preventing poaching.

Conservation organizations work to raise awareness and support initiatives to safeguard the future of these magnificent creatures.

Continued conservation efforts and community involvement are essential for the long-term survival of Siberian tigers.

INTELLIGENCE AND TOOL USE

Siberian tigers exhibit a high level of intelligence and problem-solving abilities.

They have been observed using logs or other objects as tools to reach food or create pathways.

These tigers are known to be adaptive learners, quickly adapting their hunting strategies to different prey species.

Siberian tigers display impressive memory skills, remembering the locations of prey and their territories.

They are adept at stalking and ambushing their prey, displaying patience and strategic thinking.

INTELLIGENCE AND TOOL USE

Siberian tigers have excellent spatial awareness and can navigate complex terrain with precision.

They are skilled at using camouflage and stealth to approach their prey undetected.

These tigers have the ability to learn from their experiences and adjust their behaviors accordingly.

They are known to display problem-solving skills when faced with obstacles or challenges.

Siberian tigers have been observed using their intelligence to outsmart potential predators and ensure their survival.

PREDATOR AND PREY RELATIONSHIPS

Siberian tigers are apex predators, meaning they have no natural predators in their habitat.

They play a vital role in maintaining the balance of the ecosystem by controlling prey populations.

Their main prey consists of ungulates such as deer, wild boars, and occasionally smaller mammals like hares.

Siberian tigers are known to be opportunistic hunters and will take advantage of any available food source.

They are capable of bringing down prey that is much larger than themselves, using their strength and agility.

PREDATOR AND PREY RELATIONSHIPS

Siberian tigers are skilled at ambushing their prey, using their camouflage and stealth to get close before launching an attack.

Competition for food can be fierce among tigers, and dominant individuals have priority access to the best hunting grounds.

Adult tigers require a large amount of food, with a single kill sustaining them for several days.

In some cases, Siberian tigers may scavenge on carcasses left behind by other predators.

The presence of healthy populations of prey species is crucial for the survival of Siberian tigers.

COMMUNICATION AND VOCALIZATIONS

Siberian tigers use a variety of vocalizations to communicate with other tigers, including roars, growls, hisses, and purrs.

Roaring is an important form of communication, especially during the mating season.

They also use scent markings and scratch marks on trees to communicate their presence and territorial boundaries.

Tail movements and body postures are used to convey aggression or submission to other tigers.

Vocalizations and body language are essential for maintaining social hierarchies and avoiding conflicts.

COMMUNICATION AND VOCALIZATIONS

Mothers use different vocalizations to communicate with their cubs and establish boundaries.

These tigers have a range of calls for different purposes, including warning calls to alert others to potential danger.

Male tigers may vocalize to announce their presence and assert their dominance.

Vocalizations can also be used for territorial defense and attracting mates.

The communication skills of Siberian tigers play a crucial role in their social interactions and maintaining their territories.

Unique abilities and adaptations

Siberian tigers have a unique adaptation known as a "narial" patch, which is a special gland on their upper lip that helps them mark their territory with scent.

They have excellent night vision, allowing them to hunt and navigate in low-light conditions.

Siberian tigers have large paws with retractable claws that provide them with excellent grip and traction.

Their thick fur and layer of fat help them withstand the cold temperatures of their habitat.

They have a powerful and flexible body structure, enabling them to move swiftly and silently.

Unique abilities and adaptations

Siberian tigers have a keen sense of hearing, which allows them to detect the movements of their prey.

They are skilled swimmers and can cross rivers and lakes in search of prey or to establish new territories.

Siberian tigers have adaptations that enable them to survive in harsh and snowy environments, such as dense fur and a sturdy build.

They are capable of making long leaps, allowing them to cover large distances in pursuit of prey.

Siberian tigers have the ability to go for long periods without food, conserving energy until they make a successful kill.

Made in the USA
Columbia, SC
17 July 2024

38802465R00024